Reading and Writing 1

Fall

Developed by David Reeves
for use in English for Speakers of Other Languages courses
at Chemeketa Community College

Additional contributions
by Leanne Barron and Charisa Henckel

Reading and Writing 1: Fall
ISBN: 978-1-943536-20-7
Edition 1.1 2017
© 2017 Chemeketa Community College. All rights reserved.

Chemeketa Press

Chemeketa Press is a nonprofit publishing endeavor at Chemeketa Community College. Working together with faculty, staff, and students, we develop and publish affordable and effective alternatives to commercial textbooks. All proceeds from the sale of this book will be used to develop this and other new textbooks.

Publisher: Tim Rogers
Managing Editor: Steve Richardson
Production Editor: Brian Mosher
Design Editor: Ronald Cox IV
Cover Design: Faith Martinmaas
Interior Design and Layout: Emily Evans, Faith Martinmaas, Kristi Etzel, Cierra Maher, Keyiah McClain

Acknowledgments

Image acknowledgments appear on pages 53 to 56 and constitute an extension of this copyright page.

Printed in the United States of America.

Contents

Chapter 1

Wu's Story

Wu is 35. He is from China. He was born in Shanghai. It is a big city in south China. His first language is Chinese. He moved to the USA in 2005, and he lives in Los Angeles. He is married, and he has two children, one boy and one girl. Their names are Rita and Lao. Rita is 4 and Lao is 2.

Wu's English is not very good, so he studies English. He has a class at Valley Community College. It is near his apartment. He drives to his class. He has a black 2003 Toyota Corolla. It is an old car! He is in a beginner conversation class at the college. He is in Level 1. His class is three days a week. He goes to class in the mornings because he works in the afternoon and evening. He works from 2 pm to 10 pm. He works 5 days a week. He works in a factory. He assembles windows. He is an assembler.

Exercise 1

Read Wu's story and discuss the following questions.

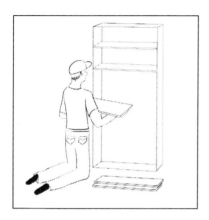 

Look at the man in the picture. He is starting to assemble the bookcase.

What does "assemble" mean?

This woman works in a factory. She is an assembler.

What does she do in her job?

Exercise 2

Copy the questions into your notebook.
Then read Wu's story and write an answer for each question.

1. What is his name?

2. Where was he born?

3. What is his first language?

4. Which city is he from?

5. When did he come to the USA?

6. How many children does he have?

7. Where does he live?

8. Does he have a car?

9. What kind of car does he have?

10. What color is his car?

11. Is he married?

12. Does he have a job?

13. Does he go to college?

14. What is his job?

15. Where does he work?

16. Does he work outside or inside?

17. What does he study at college?

18. Where does he study?

19. How does he get to college?

20. How many days a week does he have class?

21. What level is he in?

22. How many days a week does he work?

23. When does he go to college?

24. Why does he go to college in the mornings?

25. What time does he finish work?

26. How many hours a day does he work?

27. Does he speak good English?

28. How good is his English?

Exercise 3
Pronouns: he, she, it

Wu has a class at Valley Community College. It is near his apartment.

What does "it" mean? "It" = Valley Community College. "It" = something, not a person.

Where does Wu work? He works in a factory.

What does "he" mean? "He" = Wu. "He" = someone, a man or a boy.

Wu has a daughter, Rita. She doesn't go to school.

What does "she" mean? "She" = Rita. "She" = someone, a woman or a girl.

Complete the second sentence in each pair of sentences. Use *he, she* or *it.*

1. I have a car. __It__ is a Toyota Camry.
2. I work in a factory. __It__ is a big factory.
3. Jack Brown is my boss. __He__ is from Canada.
4. Sandra Ellis is my boss. __She__ is from England.
5. My teacher's name is Anita Jones. __She__ is friendly.
6. My teacher's name is Henry Smith. __He__ is a friendly person.
7. I live in an apartment. __It__ has two bedrooms.
8. I was born in Shanghai in China. __It__ is a big city.
9. My son goes to Maclean Elementary School. __It__ is near my house.
10. My wife has a job in a hotel. __She__ starts work at 10am.
11. I live in a neighborhood near Valley Community College. __It__ is a quiet part of town.

Exercise 4

My car, her car, his car, their car

Wu has a son. His name is Lao. (son = boy / male)

Wu has a daughter. Her name is Rita. (daughter = girl / female)

Jack has two children. Their names are Anna and Robert.
(two = plural)

Complete the sentences below. Use *his*, *her*, *their*.

1. I have one son. _His_ name is Alex.
2. I have one daughter. _Her_ name is Rosa.
3. I have two kids. _Their_ names are Bobby and Linda.
4. I have two sisters. _Their_ names are Patricia and Mary.
5. My son is in elementary school. _Her_ teacher is Mrs, Brown.
6. My son is in elementary school. _His_ teacher is Mr. Jackson.
7. I have two brothers. _Their_ names are Donald and Mike.
8. My sister lives in Portland. _His_ house is big.
9. Jack and Mary are married. _Their_ house is in Salem.
10. My daughter is in elementary school. _Her_ teacher is Mr. Burton.

Exercise 5
Vocabulary: occupations

Look at the pictures on the following two pages. There are 22 pictures.

In your notebook, write this question: "What is his or her job?" Then answer the question. Here are two examples:

3. What is her job? She is a teacher.
5. What is his job? He is a painter.

Choose from these occupation names:

nurse	doctor
landscaper	mail carrier
factory worker	painter
mechanic	truck driver
assembler	salesman
police officer	waiter
receptionist	taxi driver
chef	construction worker
firefighter	teacher
cleaner	hair stylist
baker	warehouse worker

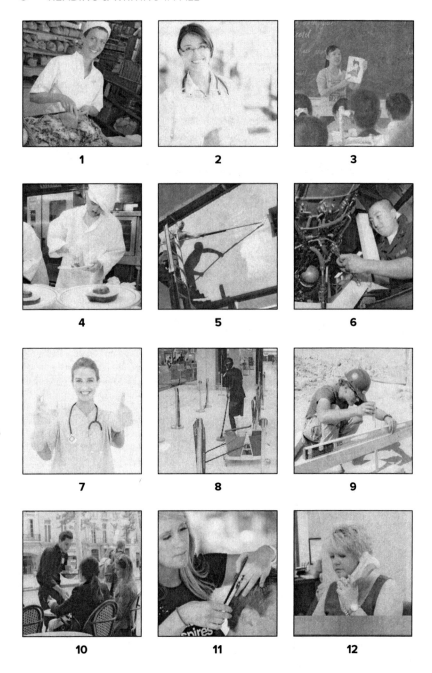

1

2

3

4

5

6

7

8

9

10

11

12

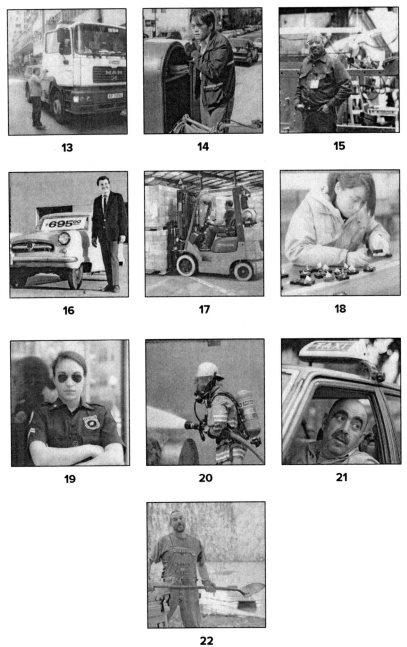

13

14

15

16

17

18

19

20

21

22

Exercise 6

The verb "have": affirmative and negative forms

Which is the true statement about Wu in the story?

> Wu _____ a car.
> a. has
> b. doesn't have

Statement **a** is true. In your notebook, write statement **a**:

> Wu has a car.

Which is the true statement about Wu in the story?

> Wu _____ a Honda Civic.
> a. has
> b. doesn't have

Statement **b** is true. In your notebook, write statement **b**:

> Wu does not have a Honda Civic.

Now read Wu's story and look at the sentences below. Which sentence is true? Write the true statements in your notebook.

1. Wu ☐ has ☐ doesn't have   three children.

2. Wu ☐ has ☐ doesn't have   English classes two days a week.

3. I ☐ have ☐ don't have   a car.

4. I ☐ have ☐ don't have   a computer at home.

5. I ☐ have ☐ don't have   a job.

6. I ☐ have ☐ don't have   an English dictionary.

7. I ☐ have ☐ don't have   a driver's license.

8. I ☐ have ☐ don't have   a bank account.

9. Wu ☐ has ☐ doesn't have   a pickup truck.

10. Wu ☐ has ☐ doesn't have   a job.

11. I ☐ have ☐ don't have   a pickup truck.

12. Wu   ☐ has ☐ doesn't have   a new car. He has an old car.

13. Wu is married.

  He   ☐ has ☐ doesn't have   two children.

14. Wu drives to college.

  He   ☐ has ☐ doesn't have   a Toyota Corolla.

Remember: I do not = I don't.
  She does not = She doesn't.
  He does not = He doesn't.

Exercise 7

Match the sentences from Column 1 with the sentences in Column 2.
Then write the sentences together in your notebook.

Column 1	Column 2
1. I type letters, and I answer the phone.	I am a salesperson.
2. I sell cars.	I am a nurse.
3. I repair cars.	I am a factory worker.
4. I take care of sick people in a hospital.	I am a receptionist.
5. I build houses.	I am a mail carrier.
6. I work in a factory. I make furniture.	I am an assembler.
7. I serve food.	I am a waiter.
8. I deliver letters and packages.	I am a construction worker.
9. I assemble windows in a factory.	I am a mechanic.
10. I load trucks, and I unload trucks in a warehouse.	I am a chef.
11. I cook food.	I am a warehouse worker.

Here is an example:

2. I sell cars. I am a salesperson.

Exercise 8
Using "a" or "an"

We use "a" before a consonant sound:

> b, c, d, f, g, h, j, k, l, m, n, p, q, r, s, t, v, w, y, z

We use "an" before a vowel sound:

> a, e, i, o, and sometimes u

The letter "u" has two different pronunciations:

> I have <u>an</u> *u*mbrella.
> He is <u>a</u> *u*niversity student.

In the sentences below, circle the correct article to use.

1. Wu lives in (a / an) apartment.
2. Wu is (a / an) student.
3. Wu is (a / an) assembler in a factory.
4. Wu has (a / an) car.
5. Wu has (a / an) old car.
6. Wu has (a / an) English class three times a week.
7. Wu isn't (a / an) American citizen.
8. Wu doesn't have (a / an) expensive car.

Exercise 9

In English, what does "Wu's car" mean? His name is Wu. "Wu's car" means that the car belongs to Wu.

We can also connect two people:

> Wu has a wife. Wu's wife is 28.
> Wu has a son. Wu's son is young.

In your notebook, use the two words to complete the sentences below. Here is an example:

> Wu / car
> <u>Wu's car</u> is black. Wu has an old car.

1. Wu / apartment

    _____ is in Los Angeles. Wu pays $600 a month for rent.

2. Wu / wife

    _____ is from China. Wu and his wife have two children.

3. Wu / children

    _____ are young. Wu takes his children to the park in

    summer.

4. Wu / job

    _____ is in a factory. Wu is an assembler.

5. Wu / car

    _____ is Japanese. Wu drives to college.

6. Wu / class

    _____ is three days a week. Wu goes to class in his car.

7. Wu / teacher

    _____ is Mrs. Anderson. Wu likes her class.

Exercise 10
Time expressions

Here are some time expressions:

five days a week   from Monday to Friday
two evenings a week   in the morning
eight hours a day   in the evening
from 8am to 4pm   in the afternoon

Step 1
Find the following sentences in Wu's story:

His class is _____ a week. He goes to class
_____ because he works _____ .

He works _____ 2pm _____ 10pm. He works
_____ a week.

Write the complete sentences in your notebook.

Step 2
Here is some information about another man. His name is Roberto
Diaz. Read the information in the table. Then complete the sentences
about Roberto in your notebook.

Roberto's activity	Days and Times
Roberto's English class	Monday and Wednesday, 8:30am – 11:30am
Roberto's job	Monday – Friday, 4pm – 10pm

Roberto has an English class at Portland Community College.
His class is _____ _____ a week. He goes to class ____ ____
_____ because he works ____ _____ _____. He works
_____ 4pm _____ 10pm. He works _____ _____ a week.

Step 3

Here is some information about a woman. Her name is Maria Gomez. Read the information in the table, and then complete the sentences about Maria in your notebook.

Maria's activity	Days and Times
Maria's class schedule	Monday, Tuesday, Wednesday, and Thursday, 6:00pm – 8:30pm
Maria's work schedule	Monday – Saturday, 6:00am – 2:00pm

Maria has an English class at Valley Community College. Her class is _____ _____ a week. She goes to class _____ _____ evening because she works _____ _____ _____. She works _____ 6am _____ 2pm. She works _____ _____ a week.

Step 4

Now complete these sentences with the correct time expression. Write the complete sentences in your notebook.

1. I usually relax _____ the evening.

2. I usually do my homework _____ the afternoon.

3. I have a part time job. I work _____ 11:30am _____ 2:30pm in a restaurant. I work three _____ a day.

4. I don't work on Monday, but I work the other days. I work _____ days _____ week.

5. I start work at 7am. I finish work at 3pm. I work eight _____ .

6. I have an English class _____ the morning because she works _____ the afternoon.

7. My sister goes to an English class _____ the morning because she works _____ the afternoon.

8. I work five days a week. I work Monday _____ Friday. I don't work on Saturday and Sunday.

Step 5
In your writing notebook, complete these sentences about yourself.

My English class is _____ a week. I go to class
_____ because I work _____ . I work from
_____ . I work _____ a week.

Exercise 11

Story 1 is Wu's story from the start of this chapter. This story is correct.

Story 1

Wu is 35. He is from China. He was born in Shanghai. It is a big city in south China. His first language is Chinese. He moved to the USA in 2005, and he lives in Los Angeles. He is married, and he has two children, one boy and one girl. Their names are Rita and Lao. Rita is 4 and Lao is 2.

Wu's English is not very good, so he studies English. He has a class at Valley Community College. It is near his apartment. He drives to his class. He has a black 2003 Toyota Corolla. It is an old car! He is in a beginner conversation class at the college. He is in Level 1. His class is three days a week. He goes to class in the mornings because he works in the afternoon and evening. He works from 2pm to 10pm. He works 5 days a week. He works in a factory. He assembles windows. He is an assembler.

There are mistakes in Story 2. Find all the differences between the information in Story 1 and Story 2.

Story 2

Wu is 36. He is from China. He was born in Shanghai. It is a big city in south China. His first language is Chinese. He moved to the USA in 2003 and he lives in Las Vegas. He is married, and he has three children, one boy and one girl. Their names are Rita and Lao. Rita is 4 and Lao is 2.

Wu's English is not very good, so he studies English. He has a class at Mesa Community College. It is near his apartment. He drives to his class. He has a black 2003 Toyota Camry. It is an old car! He is in a beginners conversation class at the college. He is in Level 2. His class is four days a week. He goes to class in the mornings because he works in the afternoon and evening. He works from 3pm to 10pm. He works 6 days a week. He works in a factory. He assembles desks for offices. He is an assembler.

Is Story 2 correct? No! There are mistakes in Story 2. Find the differences between Story 1 and Story 2. Find ten differences and write about them in your notebook.

Here is an example:

Story 2 says Wu is 36. That information is wrong! Wu is 35.

Exercise 12

Understand connections between sentences in a story and practice sentence grammar

Step 1

In your notebook, write the sentences about Wu and fill in the gaps. Don't look back at Exercise 11!

Wu is 35. He is _____ China. He was born in Shanghai. It _____ a big city in south China. His first language _____ Chinese. He moved _____ the USA in 2005, and he lives _____ Los Angeles. He _____ married, and he _____ two children, one boy and one girl. Their names _____ Rita and Lao. Rita is 4 and Lao is 2.

Wu's English is not very good, so he studies _____. _____ has a class at Valley Community College. It is near _____ apartment. He drives to his class. He _____ a black 2003 Toyota Corolla. It is an old car! He is in a beginners Conversation class at the college. _____ is in Level 1. His class _____ three days a week. He goes to class in the mornings because he works _____ the afternoon and evening. He _____ from 2pm to 10pm. He works 5 days a week. He works _____ a factory. He assembles windows. _____ is an assembler.

Step 2

In your notebook, rewrite the following sentences using correct sentence grammar, punctuation, and capitalization.

my name is Wu i am 35 i am from china i was born in shanghai it is a big city in south China my first language is chinese i moved to the USA in 2005 and i live in los angeles i am married and i have two children, one boy and one girl their names are rita and lao rita is 4 and lao is 2

my english is not very good so I attend an english class at valley community college it is near my apartment the college is about four miles from my apartment i drive to my classes i have a black 1998 toyota corolla it is old but it is a good car it doesn't have any engine problems i bought it last year from one of my friends i am in a beginners class at the college my class is a conversation class i am in Level 1 my class is three days a week there are 28 students in my class there are only three students from china we don't speak chinese in class we try to speak english all the time it is not easy my vocabulary is small i don't know many words i need to learn more vocabulary

pronunciation is also difficult for me i go to class in the mornings because I work in the afternoon and evening i work from 2pm to 10pm i work 5 days a week i work in a factory i assemble windows i am an assembler my coworkers are friendly we work hard but we have fun at work

Chapter 2
Valerie's Story

Valerie works at a motel in Portland. The motel is near the I-5 highway. The name of the motel is Days Inn. It is a big company. It has motels all over the USA. Valerie is a housekeeper. The motel employs four housekeepers. The housekeepers clean the rooms in the motel. Valerie works from 8am to 3pm. She has a lunch break from noon to 1pm. Her salary is $10 per hour. Most of the year, she works five days a week, and her days off are Tuesday and Wednesday. In summer, the motel is busy. The motel is popular with tourists. It has more guests in summer. In summer, Valerie usually works six days a week. She makes more money in summer.

Valerie cleans the motel rooms after the guests check out from their rooms. First, she changes the sheets and pillowcases on the beds. Then, she makes the beds in the room. After that, she empties all the trash cans, and she puts new trash bags in each trash can. Then, she dusts the furniture. For example, she dusts the tables, the lamps, and the TV. After that, she works in the bathroom. She needs to do a good job in all the bathrooms. Clean bathrooms are very important to motel guests. Guests complain to the manager if their bathroom is not clean. The motel manager gets angry with housekeepers if guests complain about their rooms. In the bathroom, Valerie cleans the bathtub, the toilet, and the sink. She wipes the counter around the sink, and she mops the bathroom floor. After that, she changes the towels. She puts clean towels in the bathroom. Then, she replaces the soap and shampoo. She puts new soap and shampoo on the counter. Finally, she vacuums the carpet and wipes the door handles. When she finishes a room, she locks the door and she goes to the next room.

Exercise 1

Answer these questions about Valerie's story. Write the questions and
your answers in your notebook.

1. Who is her employer?
2. Does she work for a big company or a small company?
3. What does she do?
4. Where does she work?
5. What time does she start work?
6. What time does she finish work?
7. When is her lunch break? How long is her lunch break?
8. How many housekeepers work with Valerie?
9. How many hours does she work per day?
10. How much does she earn?
11. In winter, how many days off does she have each week?
12. What are her days off in winter?
13. Is her work schedule the same all year or does her schedule
    change?
14. In summer, is the motel busy or quiet?
15. When is the motel busy? Why is it busy at that time?
16. Does Valerie clean the bedroom first, or does she clean the
    bathroom first?
17. Does she clean rooms before guests check out?
18. What does she do with the trash cans?
19. What does she do with the sheets, and the bed?
20. What does she do with the furniture?

21. What does she do with the bathroom floor?

22. What does she do with the towels?

23. What does she do with the door handles?

24. What does she do with the counter in the bathroom?

25. What does she do with the soap and shampoo?

26. What sometimes happens if the bathroom is not very clean?

Exercise 2

Write the story about Valerie in your notebook. Try to complete the sentences without looking back at the start of this chapter!

Valerie works at a _____ in Portland. The motel is near the I-5 highway. The _____ of the motel is Days Inn. It is a big company. It has motels all over the USA. Valerie _____ a housekeeper. The motel employs four housekeepers. The housekeepers _____ the rooms in the motel. Valerie _____ from 8am to 3pm. She has a lunch break _____ noon _____ 1pm. Her _____ is $10 per hour. Most of the year, she works five days a week, and her _____ _____ are Tuesday and Wednesday. In summer, the motel is _____ . The motel is popular with tourists. It has more _____ in summer. In summer, Valerie usually works six days a week. She _____ more money _____ summer.

Valerie cleans the motel rooms after the _____ check out from their rooms. First, she _____ the sheets and pillowcases on the beds. Then, she _____ the beds in the room. After that, she _____ all the trash cans, and she _____ new trash bags in each trash can. Then, she _____ the furniture. For example, she dusts the tables, the lamps, and the TV. After that, she works in the bathroom. She needs to do a good job in all the bathrooms. Clean bathrooms are very important to motel guests. Guests _____ to the manager if their bathroom is not clean. The motel _____ gets angry with housekeepers if guests complain about their rooms. In the bathroom, Valerie _____ the bathtub, the toilet, and the sink. She wipes the counter around the sink, and she mops the _____ _____. After that, she _____ the towels. She _____ clean towels in the bathroom. Then, she replaces the soap and shampoo. She puts new soap and shampoo on the _____ . Finally, she _____ the carpet and _____ the door handles. When she _____ a room, she locks the door and she goes to the next room.

Exercise 3:
Requests from your supervisor

Match actions and things in questions that a supervisor might ask. Here is an example:

> Can you <u>turn on</u> <u>the light</u> please?
>   ACTION   SOMETHING

Then write a positive response from the housekeeper. Here is an example:

> Yes, sure.

Action (= verb)	Something (= noun)
turn on	the light
lock	the counter
vacuum	all the lights
empty	the door
mop	the towels
make	the bathroom floor
change	the carpet
dust	the trash cans
replace	the sheets
wipe	the soap and shampoo
turn off	the furniture
	the bed
	the pillowcases

Use the actions and things in the table above to create questions and answers in your notebook.

a motel

guests at the motel

change the sheets

make the beds

emtpy the trash cans

dust the furniture

bathroom

towels

soap and shampoo

cleaning supplies

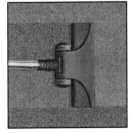

vacuum the carpet

door handle

Exercise 4

What equipment or tool do you use?

You use different tools or different equipment for different tasks at home and at work. Here is one example:

1. I   <u>cut</u>   <u>vegetables</u>   with   <u>a knife.</u>
        ACTION   SOMETHING   TOOL

Use the table below to match actions and tools like you see in the example above. Then write 15 complete sentences of your own in your notebook.

Someone + action + something	Grammar	Tool
1. I cut vegetables	with	a knife
2. I vacuum the carpet		a sponge
3. I wipe the counter		a key
4. I mop the floor		a towel
5. I lock the door		a vacuum cleaner
6. I paint the walls		a paintbrush
7. I dry my hands		a mop
8. I sweep the floor		a shovel
9. I check the temperature		a broom
10. I take photos		a camera
11. I cut paper		a thermometer
12. I climb a tree		a pair of scissors
13. I dig a hole		a spoon
14. I dry my hair		a ladder
15. I stir my coffee		a hair dryer

Exercise 5

The verb "put"

Here is and example of a sentence that uses "put" correctly:

<u>Valerie</u>   <u>puts</u>   <u>clean sheets</u> <u>on the bed</u>.
SOMEONE ACTION   SOMETHING   SOMEWHERE

Here is the same sentence in a table:

Someone (= noun)	Action (= verb)	Something (= noun)	Somewhere (= place noun)
Valerie	puts	clean sheets	on the bed

Now look at the jumbled sentences below.

1. clean sheets / Valerie / the bed / on / puts

2. new trash bags / the trash cans / Valerie / in / puts

3. the counter / Valerie / on / new soap and shampoo / in the bathroom / puts

4. puts / Valerie / the pillows / clean pillowcases / on

5. the washer / I / in / my dirty clothes / put

6. the wet clothes / put / the dryer / I / in

7. fresh water / a bottle / put / I / in

8. the refrigerator / fresh vegetables / put / in / I

Copy the table below into your notebook. Then use the table to write 8 good sentences like you see above.

Someone (= noun)	Action (= verb)	Something (= noun)	Somewhere (= place noun)

Exercise 6

Practice sentence grammar

In your notebook, rewrite the following sentences using correct sentence grammar, punctuation, and capitalization.

valerie works at a motel in portland the motel is near the i-5 highway the name of the motel is days inn it is a big company it has motels all over the usa valerie is a housekeeper the motel employs four housekeepers the housekeepers clean the rooms in the motel valerie works from 8am to 3pm she has a lunch break from noon to 1pm her salary is $10 per hour most of the year she works five days a week and her days off are tuesday and wednesday in summer the motel is busy the motel is popular with tourists it has more guests in summer in summer valerie usually works six days a week she makes more money in summer

valerie cleans the motel rooms after the guests check out from their rooms first she changes the sheets and pillowcases on the beds then, she makes the beds in the room after that she empties all the trash cans and she puts new trash bags in each trash can then she dusts the furniture for example she dusts the tables the lamps and the tv after that she works in the bathroom she needs to do a good job in all the bathrooms clean bathrooms are very important to motel guests guests complain to the manager if their bathroom is not clean the motel manager gets angry with housekeepers if guests complain about their rooms in the bathroom valerie cleans the bathtub the toilet and the sink she wipes the counter around the sink and she mops the bathroom floor after that she changes the towels she puts clean towels in the bathroom then she replaces the soap and shampoo she puts new soap and shampoo on the counter finally she vacuums the carpet and wipes the door handles when she finishes a room she locks the door and she goes to the next room

Chapter 3
Patricia's Story

Patricia works at a bakery. She bakes cakes, pies, and cookies. The name of the bakery is CakeTime. The bakery is a popular and successful business. It gets a lot of special orders. For example, the bakery makes a lot of wedding cakes and birthday cakes. The owner of the bakery is Mrs Jefferson. She started the business thirty years ago, but she doesn't work at the bakery now. She's 71, and she has health problems. Mrs. Jefferson's daughter, Sylvia, is the manager at the bakery.

Patricia started work at CakeTime four years ago. The bakery opens early in the morning. It opens at 7:15am, six days a week. The bakery is very busy around breakfast time. Many people want coffee, donuts, and muffins for breakfast. The bakery makes a lot of money at breakfast time. Patricia and the other kitchen workers have to make the donuts and muffins before 7am, so they start work at 5am. When they finish the donuts and muffins, the kitchen workers make bread, cakes, pies, and cookies. Patricia makes pies, cakes, and cookies. She doesn't make bread.

At lunch time, the bakery sells a lot of sandwiches. The bakery is downtown, and there are a lot of office buildings in the area. The bakery is a popular place for office workers at lunch time. A lot of office workers come to the bakery at lunch time to buy sandwiches for lunch. In the afternoon, the bakery sells a lot of bread, cakes and pies. There are a lot of stores in the downtown area. Many people go shopping, and then they go to the bakery in the afternoon for a snack, or for coffee, or to meet their friends.

Patricia and the other employees in the kitchen get off work at 2pm. Before they finish work, the kitchen workers clean up the kitchen. For example, they wash the appliances, and they put away all the food items. They put all the fresh food in the refrigerators, and they put all the dry food (flour, sugar, etc) in the cabinets or on the shelves. The employees who serve customers don't have the same work hours. They work from 7am to 4:15pm. The bakery closes at 4pm. The bakery is open six days a week. It is closed on Sundays.

Patricia is married, and she has two children. The children go to elementary school. Patricia picks up her kids at school at 2:30pm. In the morning, Patricia cannot take the kids to school because she starts work very early. Her husband, Alex, starts work at 9am, so he drops off the kids at school on his way to work.

Exercise 1

Answer these questions about Patricia's story. Write the questions and your answers in your notebook.

1. What does Patricia do for a living?
2. Is she a cashier in a bakery?
3. Is she a baker?
4. Does she work in a kitchen?
5. Who is her employer?
6. Is Patricia an employer or an employee?
7. Does Patricia bake bread?
8. Does she make cakes?
9. A. What time does she start work?

   B. Why does she start work very early in the morning?
10. What time does she finish work?
11. Do all the employees at CakeTime have the same work schedule?
12. What time does the bakery open?
13. What are the business hours of the bakery?
14. Who owns the bakery?
15. Is CakeTime a new business?
16. Why do a lot of office workers go to the bakery to buy sandwiches?
17. What items are popular at breakfast time?
18. In the morning, what do the kitchen workers make first?
19. At breakfast time, does the bakery have a lot of customers?
20. Does the bakery make sandwiches?
21. When does the bakery sell a lot of sandwiches?

22. Who is the bakery manager?

23. When does Patricia make cakes and pies?

24. Does the bakery sell coffee?

25. Does the bakery have financial problems?

26. Is Patricia an office worker?

27. Can people buy birthday cakes at CakeTime?

28. When does the bakery sell a lot of cakes and pies?

29. When did Patricia start work at CakeTime?

30. Does Patricia take her kids to school in the morning?

31. Does Patricia pick up her kids at school in the afternoon?

Exercise 2
Positive or negative **verb** + a lot of + **something**

Verbs	Nouns (Things)
have, don't have, doesn't have, had, has, use, make, makes, don't make, doesn't make, eats, earns, does, do, don't do, didn't have, sells, works	books, sugar, mistakes, money, fun, employees, accidents, cakes and pies, students, traffic, cars, overtime, nice stores, apples and oranges, sandwiches, noise, customers, homework

From the table above, choose one verb (action) and one noun (thing) to complete the following sentences. For example, you read this:

> I like sweet coffee. I _____ a lot of _____.

Then you write this in your notebook:

> I like sweet coffee. I use a lot of sugar.

Complete all the sentences in your notebook.

1. I like reading. I _____ a lot of _____ at my house.

2. He likes fruit. He _____ a lot of _____ .

3. I don't like reading. I _____ a lot of _____ .

4. She is rich. She _____ a lot of _____ .

5. They are poor. They _____ a lot of _____ .

6. She has a good job. She _____ a lot of _____ .

7. I don't speak English very well. I _____ a lot of _____ .

8. My sister's English is very good . She _____ a lot of _____.

9. He works 12 hours a day. He _____ a lot of _____ .

10. This class is very hard work. The students _____ a lot of

    _____ .

11. This class is very easy. The students _____ a lot of ____ .

12. The children are quiet. They _____ a lot of _____ .

13. I enjoyed my vacation last month. I _____ a lot of _____ .

14. I like my math class. It _____ a lot of _____ .

15. I don't like my new English class. It _____ a lot of _____ .

16. This street is very dangerous. This street _____ a lot of

    _____ .

17. My class is very small. The class _____ a lot of _____ .

18. My class is very big. The class _____ a lot of _____ .

19. This street is very quiet. This street _____ a lot of ____ .

20. He is a lazy student. He _____ a lot of _____ .

21. This restaurant is very popular. It _____ a lot of _____ .

22. The food at this bakery is very good. The bakery _____ a lot

    of _____ .

23. This company is very successful. It _____ a lot of _____ .

24. The bakery is near a lot of offices. At lunchtime, the bakery

    _____ a lot of_____ to office workers.

25. This company is very big. It _____ a lot of _____ .

26. I like this part of Portland. I like shopping. This area _____ a

    lot of _____ .

Exercise 3

Put these actions from Patricia's story into the correct order. The first step is 1. The second step is 2. And so on.

1. The bakery closes.

2. The bakery opens for customers.

3. The kitchen workers start to make donuts and muffins.

4. The kitchen workers finish work.

5. The kitchen workers start work.

6. Some employees start to make pies.

7. The food servers start work.

8. The food servers get off work.

9. The kitchen workers clean the kitchen area.

Write your list of sentences in your notebook.

Exercise 4

Same meaning

Replace the underlined words of the sentences in first column with words or phrases from the second column that have the same meaning. Write both sentences in your notebook. Here is one example:

10. My class starts at 9am. = My class begins at 9am.

1.	The <u>bakery is open</u> from 7:15am to 4pm.	I don't work on
2.	Patricia <u>started work</u> at Cake Time 4 years ago.	have different work schedules
3.	Patricia <u>gets off</u> work at 2pm.	The bakery's business hours are
4.	The bakery <u>is closed</u> on Sundays.	shut off
5.	<u>My day off is</u> Sunday.	finishes
6.	The bakery <u>closes</u> at 4pm.	makes
7.	Food servers and kitchen workers <u>don't have the same work hours.</u>	drop off her children at
8.	Do you want me to <u>turn off</u> the oven?	got a job
9.	Patricia <u>bakes</u> pies.	doesn't open
10.	My class <u>starts</u> at 9am.	wear
11.	Kitchen workers need to <u>use a</u> hairnet in the kitchen.	begins
12.	Patricia doesn't <u>take her kids</u> to school in the morning.	shuts
13.	I <u>earn</u> $11 per hour.	makes a lot of money
14.	This restaurant <u>isn't popular.</u>	make
15.	This store <u>is successful.</u>	doesn't get a lot of customers

Exercise 5
Use "a lot of" in the subject noun of a sentence

This is the grammar for the sentences with "a lot of" that you saw in Exercise 2 and 4.

Subject Noun of the Sentence (Someone or Something)	Verb	Another Noun (Someone or Something)	More information (if necessary)
My brother This class	has doesn't have	a lot of books a lot of donuts a lot of students	in the morning.

In English, we can also use a lot of at the beginning of the sentence with the subject noun. Here's one example:

Subject Noun of the Sentence (Someone or Something)	Verb	Another Noun (Someone or Something)	More information (if necessary)
A lot of students	use	laptop computers.	

On the next page, combine one sentence from the first column with another related sentence from the second column. Then write the combinations in your notebook. Here is one example:

1. Laptop computers are very popular in colleges.

   A lot of students use them.

   (Subject of Sentence 2)

Sentence 1	Sentence 2
1. Laptop computers are very popular in colleges.	A lot of office workers buy sandwiches from the bakery.
2. The CakeTime Bakery is downtown near a lot of office buildings.	A lot of students use them.
3. The CakeTime Bakery makes wedding cakes and birthday cakes.	A lot of people like it.
4. Traffic is very slow in this part of the city between 7am and 10am.	A lot of people like them.
5. At the CakeTime Bakery, donuts are popular in the morning.	A lot of people order them.
6. This English class is very popular.	A lot of people ride them.
7. This parking lot is usually full.	A lot of people drive to work.
8. This music is very popular.	A lot of people use it.
9. Bicycles are very popular in Portland.	A lot of people use them.
10. The pies at this bakery are good.	A lot of people buy them for breakfast.
11. Cell phones are very common now.	A lot of drivers drive too fast.
12. Vitamin pills are popular in USA.	A lot of people take it every term.
13. The streets in the city are dangerous for people on bicycles.	A lot of cyclists use bike helmets.
14. I see a lot of accidents on this street.	A lot of people take them.

Exercise 6

Instructions and locations

In the picture below, there are three shelves, the top shelf, the middle shelf, and the bottom shelf.

Which shelf is the top shelf? Which shelf is the bottom shelf? Which shelf is the middle shelf?

top shelf
middle shelf
bottom shelf

Now turn the next page and follow the instructions.

Create a set of three shelves like this in your notebook.

Now follow the instructions and draw each item on the correct shelf.

1. Put the bag of flour on the middle shelf please.

2. Put the cans of tuna fish on the bottom shelf please.

3. Put the box of salt on the top shelf please.

4. Put the cans of soup on the bottom shelf please.

5. Put the packet of tea on the top shelf please.

6. Put the bag of black pepper on the middle shelf please.

Exercise 7

Vocabulary

In your notebook, write the name of each item and then the correct number from the pictures. Some pictures work for more than one item.

measuring spoons	a piece of pie	a cash register
a box of donuts	a display counter	a plate
a bakery worker	a measuring cup	
a wedding cake	the top shelf	

1   2   3

4   5   6

7   8

Exercise 8

Vocabulary

In your notebook, write the name of each item and then the correct number from the pictures. Some pictures work for more than one item.

coffee maker	teapot	measuring spoons	cup of tea
toaster	blender	paper towels	stove
food mixer	loaf of bread	scale	top shelf
measuring cup	slice of bread	bowl	counter
can opener	piece of toast	bakery worker	pan
rolling pin	tea cup	book of recipes	frying pan

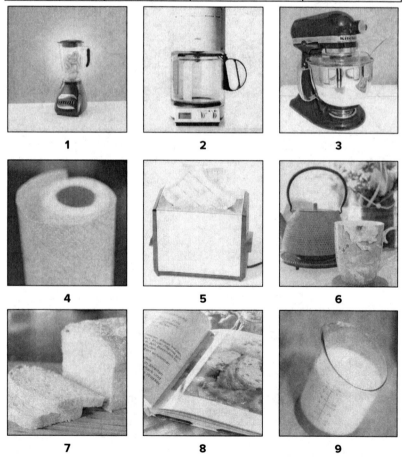

1

2

3

4

5

6

7

8

9

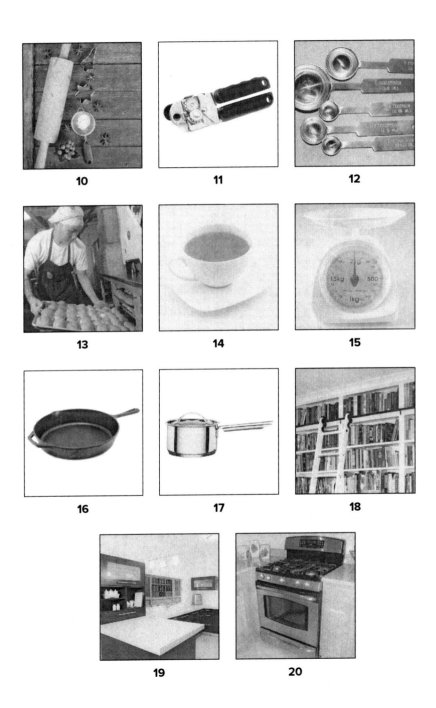

10

11

12

13

14

15

16

17

18

19

20

Exercise 9

Kitchen tasks

How do you do these tasks? What tools do you use? Match up the questions and correct answers from the table below.

Question	Short Answer
1. How do you boil an egg?	With a knife.
2. Where do you make toast?	In a food mixer.
3. Where do you bake pies?	In a pan of water.
4. How do you make a	In a blender.
milk shake?	In a pan on the stove.
5. How do you fry chicken?	In oil in a frying pan.
6. How do you warm up a can	On a scale.
of soup?	With a spoon.
7. How do you open a can	In a big bowl.
of tuna?	In a toaster.
8. How do you cut bread?	With a can opener.
9. How do you serve salad to	In an oven.
your family?	
10. Where do you mix the	
ingredients for a cake?	
11. How do you eat cereal?	
12. How do you weigh the fruit?	

Write each question and the correct short answer in your notebook. Here is an example:

11. How do you eat cereal? With a spoon.

Exercise 10
Vocabulary: What does "put away" mean?

Before Patricia and the other kitchen workers go home, they put away all the equipment and all the food in the correct place for each thing.

"Put away" means to put something in the correct place. In your house, is the refrigerator the correct place to put your shoes? No! Where is the correct place to put your shoes? Usually, "put away" means to "put your shoes in the closet in your bedroom".

Where is the correct place to put these things? In your notebook, write each "put away" sentence from the first column of the table on the next page. Then choose the correct place to put it from the second column and write what "put away" means. Here is an example:

4.   Put away the books on the floor.
     Answer: It means put them in the bookcase.

Turn the page for the table of things to put away.

Somebody says this to you:	Put away means to...
1. Put away your jacket please.	put it in the garage
2. Put away the ice cream please.	put them in the bookcase
3. Put away the milk please.	put it in your wallet
4. Put away the books on the floor.	put it in the closet
5. Put away your books before I give you the test.	put it in your purse
6. Jack, put away your credit card.	put them on the shelf next to the refrigerator
7. Put away the cans of tuna from the store.	put them in the medicine cabinet in the bathroom
8. Put away your clean socks please.	put them in your bag or backpack
9. Put away the lawn mower please.	put it in the freezer
10. Put away the big pan please.	put them in the kitchen cabinet next to the sink
11. Put away the aspirin please. I don't want the baby to eat some!	put them in the dresser in your bedroom
12. Put away the clean plates please.	put it in the refrigerator
13. Mary, put away your credit card.	put it on the shelf next to the stove

Exercise 11
Adjectives and nouns

Adjectives give more information about nouns (things or people).
Adjectives describe nouns. Here is an example:

> Jack: "I live on Madison Street."
> Mary: "What kind of street is it? "
> Jack: "It is a <u>quiet</u> street. It is not a <u>busy</u> street."

	Adjective = description word	Noun = something or someone
a	quiet	street
not a	busy	street
a	busy	teacher

Now write sensible adjective + noun combinations of your own. Choose adjectives from the Adjective column and match them with nouns from the Noun column. Write the combinations in your notebook.

		Adjective	Noun
	1.	sharp	temperature
	2.	heavy	knife
	3.	quiet	shelf
	4.	high	restaurant
	5.	bright	lunch break
a	6.	long	street
	7.	dirty	floor
	8.	successful	piece of butter
	9.	short	food mixer
	10.	wet	light
	11.	hard	box

Exercise 12

Time expressions

At

at + one specific time point, one specific clock time

Here are some examples: at 8:30pm, at lunch time, at dinner time, at breakfast time, at break time.

From ___ to ___

from ___ to ___ + two time expressions

Here are some examples: from 8:30pm to 10pm, from 1990 to 2007, from January 2014 to September 2016, from Monday to Friday.

On

on + a day, days, or part of a day

Here are some examples: on Tuesday, on Christmas, on my birthday, on Tuesday morning, on Tuesday afternoon, on Friday night, on work days, on school days, on May 14 (May 14 is a day.).

In

in + month name

Here are some examples: in June, in September.

in + a year or set of years

Here are some examples: in 2016, in the 1990s.

in + a season

Here are some examples: in summer, in winter, in spring.

in + a part of the day

Here are some examples: in the morning, in the afternoon.

Complete the sentences below with *at, on, in,* or *from ___ to ___*. Write the complete sentences in your notebook.

1. The bakery opens _____ 7:15am.

2. Patricia starts work _____ 5am.

3. Patricia works _____ 5am _____ 2pm.

4. Patricia doesn't work _____ Sunday.

5. Patricia works _____ Monday _____ Saturday.

6. The bakery is busy _____ the morning.

7. Patricia's husband takes their kids to school _____ the morning.

8. Patricia's husband doesn't need to take their kids to school _____ Saturday.

9. The bakery is busy _____ noon _____ 1:30pm. This is lunchtime for many people.

10. The bakery is not open _____ the evening.

11. The bakery is open _____ 7:15am _____ 4pm.

12. The bakery closes _____ 4pm.

13. I have an English class _____ Monday.

14. I have a math class _____ Tuesday morning.

15. My class _____ Tuesday starts _____ 9am.

16. I don't have a class _____ Wednesday.

17. I don't have a class _____ Tuesday afternoon.

18. My birthday is _____ July.

19. My birthday is _____ July 17th.

20. I was born _____ 1986.

21. I have a vacation _____ summer.

22. It is cold _____ winter.

23. I need to talk to you _____ break time.

24. I go to bed _____ 11pm _____ workdays.

25. I do my homework _____ the evening after dinner.

26. The restaurant is busy _____ breakfast time.

27. I started to work at this bakery _____ 2006.

Acknowledgments

The chapters in this book incorporate images from the following sources.

Figure 1. "Man assembling bookcase" by Emily Evans is a product of work by Chemeketa Visual Communications Program and Chemeketa Press.

Figure 2. "Seagate Wuxi China Factory Tour" by Robert Scoble is licensed under CC BY 2.0 (https://commons.wikimedia.org/wiki/File:-Seagate_Wuxi_China_Factory_Tour.jpg).

Figure 3. "Baker Oslo" by Thomas Berg is licensed under CC BY-SA 2.0 (https://commons.wikimedia.org/wiki/File:Baker_Oslo.jpg).

Figure 4. "bodycare, clinic, clipboard, doc, doctor, female," by Ilmicrofono Oggiono is licensed under CC BY 2.0 (https://www.flickr.com/photos/115089924@N02/16070083419).

Figure 5. "Student teacher in China" by Adrignola is licensed under CC BY 2.0 (https://commons.wikimedia.org/wiki/File:Student_teacher_in_China.jpg).

Figure 6. "n/a" by skeeze is licensed under CC0 Public Domain (https://pixabay.com/en/chefs-competition-cooking-749563/).

Figure 7. "n/a" by christianluiz18 is licensed under CC0 Public Domain (https://pixabay.com/en/paint-painting-painter-green-wall-231726/).

Figure 8. "US Navy 041111-N-2143T-013 Aviation Structural Mechanic 2nd Class Chou Yang of Braselton, Ga., installs drain lines on the afterburner of an F-414 aircraft engine aboard USS Nimitz (CVN 68)" by U.S. Navy photo by Airman Maebel Tinoko is licensed under CC0 Public Domain (https://commons.wikimedia.org/wiki/File:US_Navy_041111-N-2143T-013_Aviation_Structural_Mechanic_2nd_Class_Chou_Yang_of_Braselton,_Ga.,_installs_drain_lines_on_the_afterburner_of_an_F-414_aircraft_engine_aboard_USS_Nimitz_(CVN_68).jpg).

Figure 9. "Amused brown haired nurse in blue scrubs giving a thumb up while holding a glass of water on white b" by Aqua Mechanical is licensed under CC BY 2.0 (https://www.flickr.com/photos/aquamech-utah/24978997901).

Figure 10. "Cleaner on airport Sri Lanka" by Peter van der Sluijs is licensed under CC BY-SA 3.0, CC BY-SA 2.5, CC BY-SA 2.0, CC BY-SA 1.0 (https://commons.wikimedia.org/wiki/File:-Cleaner_on_airport_Sri_Lanka.JPG).

Figure 11. "US Navy 080606-N-9623R-414 Builder 2nd Class Kathryn Henderson, assigned to Naval Mobile Construction Battalion (NMCB) 3, uses a horizontal level and tape measure" by U.S. Navy photo by Mass Communication Specialist 2nd Class Kenneth W. Robinson is licensed under CC0 Public Domain (https://commons.wikimedia.org/wiki/File:US_Navy_080606-N-9623R-414_Builder_2nd_Class_Kathryn_Henderson,_assigned_to_Naval_Mobile_Construction_Battalion_(NMCB)_3,_uses_a_horizontal_level_and_tape_measure.jpg).

Figure 12. "Our waiter." by Connie Ma is licensed under CC BY-SA 2.0 (https://www.flickr.com/photos/ironypoisoning/14096081640).

Figure 13. "Paul Mitchell Hair Stylist" by Michael Dorausch is licensed under CC BY-SA 2.0 (https://www.flickr.com/photos/chiropractic/6070427981).

Figure 14. "receptionist answering phone at suburban eye care" by John Jacobi is licensed under CC BY 2.0 (https://www.flickr.com/photos/suburbaneyecare/7269959082).

Figure 15. "HK Shek Tong Tsui Des Voeux Road West Bus KMB MAN FE360 A" by SunTsiuKee111 is licensed under CC BY-SA 3.0 (https://commons.wikimedia.org/wiki/File:HK_Shek_Tong_Tsui_Des_Voeux_Road_West_Bus_KMB_MAN_FE360_A.JPG).

Figure 35. "Cleaning" by NY - http://nyphoto-graphic.com/ is licensed under CC BY-SA 3.0 (http://www.picserver.org/c/cleaning.html).

Figure 36. "Vacuum Cleaner" by jarmoluk is licensed under CC0 Public Domain (https://pixabay.com/p-268179/?no_redirect).

Figure 37. "door handle" by khairul nizam is licensed under CC0 Public Domain (https://www.pexels.com/photo/door-doorknob-door-knob-door-handle-16515/).

Figure 38. "Library Bookshelf" by Open Grid Scheduler is licensed under CC0 Public Domain (https://www.flickr.com/photos/opengridscheduler/22468805072).

Figure 39. "Wedding cake pale roses" by Linda Marklund is licensed under CC BY 2.0 (https://www.flickr.com/photos/51226001@N03/8116588363).

Figure 40. "Box of donuts" by anya1 is licensed under CC0 Public Domain (https://pixabay.com/p-179248/?no_redirect).

Figure 41. "Pumpkin Pie Slice (5076305261)" by TheCulinaryGeek is licensed under CC BY 2.0 (https://commons.wikimedia.org/wiki/File:Pumpkin_Pie_Slice_(5076305261).jpg).

Figure 42. "Measuring Spoons" by Julie Magro is licensed under CC BY 2.0 (https://www.flickr.com/photos/magro-fami-ly/4601000979).

Figure 43. "ISI Measuring Cup" by Didriks is licensed under CC BY 2.0 (https://www.flickr.com/photos/dinnerseries/9919941506).

Figure 44. "Bakery worker" by Unsplash is licensed under CC0 Public Domain (https://www.pexels.com/photo/market-bread-wom-en-amish-34035/).

Figure 45. "Bakery display case" by Unsplash is licensed under CC0 Public Domain (https://pixabay.com/p-1209446/?no_redirect).

Figure 45b. "Cash register" by bladerunner1968 is licensed under CC0 Public Domain (https://pixabay.com/p-812861/?no_redirect).

Figure 46. "Blender" by opaye is licensed under CC0 Public Domain (https://pixabay.com/p-10934/?no_redirect).

Figure 47. "Braun Coffee Maker" by Austin Calhoon is licensed under CC BY-SA 3.0 (https://commons.wikimedia.org/wiki/File:Braun_Coffee_Maker.jpg).

Figure 48. "Black KitchenAid Mixer" by Warren Layton is licensed under CC BY 2.0 (https://commons.wikimedia.org/wiki/File:Black_KitchenAid_Mixer.jpg).

Figure 49. "Fat Spiral" by J. Ott is licensed under CC BY 2.0 (https://www.flickr.com/photos/thousandshipz/4519556125).

Figure 50. "Toaster And Slices Of Bread" by yamada taro is licensed under CC0 Public Domain (http://www.publicdomainpictures.net/view-image.php?image=26196).

Figure 51. "Empty Teacup" by Humusak is licensed under CC0 Public Domain (https://pixabay.com/p-549084/?no_redirect).

Figure 52. "Anadama bread (1)" by Stacy is licensed under CC BY 2.0 (https://commons.wikimedia.org/wiki/File:Anadama_bread_(1).jpg).

Figure 53. "Recipe book" by Romi is licensed under CC0 Public Domain (https://pixabay.com/p-746005/?no_redirect).

Figure 54. "Oxo measuring cup" by Didriks is licensed under CC BY 2.0 (https://www.flickr.com/photos/dinnerseries/20579081940).

Figure 55. "rolling pin with measuring cup and cookie cutter on dark wooden crate" by Personal Creations is licensed under CC BY 2.0 (https://www.flickr.com/photos/personal-creations/26749955511).

Figure 56. "Kitchen-Modern-Can-Opener" by Evan-Amos is licensed under CC0 Public Domain (https://commons.wikimedia.org/wiki/File:Kitchen-Modern-Can-Opener.jpg).

Figure 57. "Measuring spoons" by handikapinfo is licensed under CC0 Public Domain (https://pixabay.com/p-1208455/?no_redirect).

Figure 58. "USS John C. Stennis baker" by Petty Officer 3rd Class Paul J. Perkins, U.S. Navy is licensed under CC0 Public Domain (https://commons.wikimedia.org/wiki/File:USS_John_C._Stennis_baker.jpg).

Figure 59. "Cup Of Tea Isolated" by Petr Kratochvil is licensed under CC0 Public Domain (http://www.publicdomainpictures.net/view-image.php?image=4291).

Figure 60. "Kitchen scale 20101110" by Batholith is licensed under CC0 Public Domain (https://commons.wikimedia.org/wiki/File:Kitchen_scale_20101110.jpg).

Figure 61. "Cast-Iron-Pan" by Evan-Amos is licensed under CC0 Public Domain (https://commons.wikimedia.org/wiki/File:Cast-Iron-Pan.jpg).

Figure 62. "Hahn 16cm Saucepan" by Cooks & Kitchens is licensed under CC BY 2.0 (https://commons.wikimedia.org/wiki/File:Hahn_16cm_Saucepan.jpg).

Figure 63. "Bookcase with ladder- still not organized!" by Robin Zebrowski is licensed under CC BY 2.0 (https://www.flickr.com/photos/firepile/4226917712).

Figure 64. "Modern-sleek-kitchen-counter-tops stonetopgranite 4" by Stonetopgranite is licensed under CC BY-SA 4.0 (https://commons.wikimedia.org/wiki/File:Modern-sleek-kitchen-counter-tops_stonetopgranite_4.jpg).

Figure 65. "GE Profile stove" by BrokenSphere is licensed under CC BY-SA 3.0, CC BY-SA 2.5, CC BY-SA 2.0, CC BY-SA 1.0 (https://commons.wikimedia.org/wiki/File:GE_Profile_stove.JPG).

Figure 66. "Fridge minsk2" by Atlantbt is licensed under CC BY-SA 4.0 (https://commons.wikimedia.org/wiki/File:Fridge_minsk2.jpg).

Figure 67. "Shoes" by Web Donut is licensed under CC0 Public Domain (https://www.pexels.com/photo/fashion-shoes-footwear-19090/).

Figure 68. "Walk In Closet - Expandable Closet Rod and Shelf" by Wjablow is licensed under CC BY-SA 3.0 (https://commons.wikimedia.org/wiki/File:Walk_In_Closet_-_Expandable_Closet_Rod_and_Shelf.jpg).

Figure 69. "Alarm Clocks 20101107a" by Batholith is licensed under CC0 Public Domain (https://commons.wikimedia.org/wiki/File:Alarm_Clocks_20101107a.jpg).

Figure 70. "Untitled" by GDJ is licensed under CC0 Public Domain (https://pixabay.com/en/calendar-date-month-year-time-1301748/).

CPSIA information can be obtained
at www.ICGtesting.com
Printed in the USA
FSOW02n2344280817
37936FS